Science Ethics
and Controversies

Eve Hartman and Wendy Meshbesher

Raintree

Chicago, Illinois

www.heinemannraintree.com
Visit our website to find out more information about Heinemann-Raintree books.

To order:
☎ Phone 888-454-2279
🖳 Visit www.heinemannraintree.com to browse our catalog and order online.

Edited by Adam Miller, Andrew Farrow, and Adrian Vigliano
Designed by Philippa Jenkins and Ken Vail
Original illustrations © Capstone Global Library Limited 2009
Illustrated by Ian Escott
Picture research by Ruth Blair
Originated by Raintree
Printed and bound in China by South China Printing Company Ltd.

13 12 11 10 09
10 9 8 7 6 5 4 3 2 1

Library of Congress Cataloging-in-Publication Data
Hartman, Eve.
  Science ethics and controversies / Eve Hartman and Wendy Meshbesher.
    p. cm. -- (Sci-hi. Life science)
  Includes bibliographical references and index.
  ISBN 978-1-4109-3330-0 (hc) -- ISBN 978-1-4109-3338-6 (pb) 1. Research--Moral and ethical aspects--Juvenile literature. 2. Science--Moral and ethical aspects--Juvenile literature. 3. Science--Social aspects--Juvenile literature. I. Meshbesher, Wendy. II. Title.
  Q180.55.M67H375 2008
  174'.95--dc22
                         2009003475

Acknowledgments
The authors and publishers are grateful to the following for permission to reproduce copyright material: Alamy/Amana Images Inc. pp. **6**, **13**, /John Angerson p. **21**, /Arctic Images p. **40**, /Nick Duff Davies p. **22**, /DBURKE p. **37**, /Paul Andrew Lawrence p. **23**, /Oliver Leedham p. **17**, /David L. Moore-Lifestyle p. **19**; CORBIS/Holberman Collection p. **14** (bottom), /Dana Neely p. **25**; Getty Images/Harrison; Hulton Archive p. **18**; iStockphoto/ p. **28**, Mark Evans pp. **3** (top),**16**, Cathy Keifer p. **8**, **8**, Hans Laubel p. **36**, James Steidl p. **34**; NASA/ pp. **3** (bottom), **31**; PA Photos/AP Photo; David J. Philip p. **38**; PA Photos/AP Photo; Northern Wyoming Daily News, Jilaena Childs p. **32**; Photolibrary Group/nonstock p. **14** (top); REUTERS/ Eduardo Munoz p. **30**; Science Photo Library/ pp. **5** (bottom), **11**, Andrew Brookes, National Physical Laboratory p. **35**, David R. Frazier pp. **20**, **41**, Adam Gault p. **17**, NOAA p. **5** (top), Sam Ogden pp. **24**, **26**, Royal Astronomical Society p. **29**, Sheila Terry p. **29**; Shutterstock/ background images and design features.

Cover photograph of a gene-modified mouse on a DNA sequence graph reproduced with permission of Alamy/ © Deco Images II. **main**: Cover photograph of a computer-enhanced nuclear explosion from original US government black and white image reproduced with permission of Alamy/ © PHOTOTAKE Inc. **inset**.

The publishers would like to thank literacy consultant Nancy Harris for her assistance in the preparation of this book.

Every effort has been made to contact copyright holders of any material reproduced in this book. Any omissions will be rectified in subsequent printings if notice is given to the publisher.

All the Internet addresses (URLs) given in this book were valid at the time of going to press. However, due to the dynamic nature of the Internet, some addresses may have changed, or sites may have changed or ceased to exist since publication. While the author and Publishers regret any inconvenience this may cause readers, no responsibility for any such changes can be accepted by either the author or the Publishers.

Contents

Does this airplane bring benefits or drawbacks?

Find out on page 16!

Where are these astronauts?

Find out on page 31!

Some words are shown in bold, **like this**. These words are explained in the glossary. You will find important information and definitions underlined, <u>like this</u>.

Issues and Controversies

Science is always in the news. On any given day, you might hear about doctors studying a new medicine, engineers investigating an old bridge, or astronomers looking for new objects in space. A story about a hurricane could bring opinions from **meteorologists**, environmental scientists, and health and safety experts.

Scientists make discoveries, develop new technologies, and study events in nature that affect everyone. For this reason, the work of scientists is often controversial, meaning that people have different opinions about it. This book will explain some of the ways these ethical issues (questions of what is right and wrong) and controversies happen.

The power of evidence

In 1912, German scientist Alfred Wegener proposed an explanation for the shape of Earth's continents. Wegener argued that the continents were once joined together. Then they slowly drifted apart to their current locations.

The experts of the time questioned Wegener. They could not imagine how continents could move, and Wegener could not answer their questions.

Yet in the 1950s, scientists began studying the floor of the Atlantic Ocean. They discovered a mountain range in the middle of the ocean floor. The range was in the same shape as the coastlines of Africa and South America, and was **evidence** that Wegener was correct. Evidence is any observable fact from nature.

<u>Throughout the history of science, new evidence has helped topple old ideas in favor of new ones.</u> Today, all scientists accept the idea that sections of Earth slowly move across the surface.

To Alfred Wegener, matching coastlines were evidence that the continents were once joined together. Today, a huge body of evidence shows this idea to be correct. Look at the map. Can you see how the continents might have once fit together?

THE SCIENTIFIC METHOD

How can weeds be killed without harming other plants? Where will the next severe earthquake strike? What objects orbit the Sun beyond Pluto? Scientists investigate questions like these every day.

For each question or topic, scientists apply the same method of investigation. **The scientific method is a system of observation, experimentation, and analysis that leads to logical conclusions.** Another name for the scientific method is **science inquiry**. Its steps are described in this chapter.

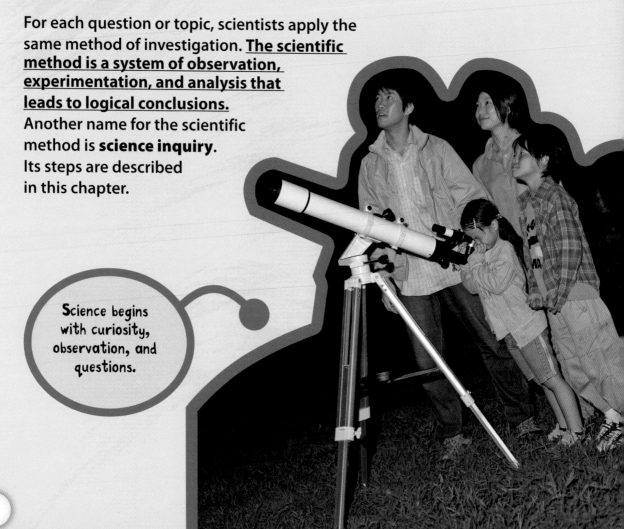

Science begins with curiosity, observation, and questions.

Observing and questioning

If you observed a caterpillar over time, you would see it spin a cocoon. Continue observing, and you would see a butterfly emerge. But what happens inside the cocoon? Just how does a caterpillar change?

Making observations and asking questions are the first two steps of the scientific method. If you ever wondered about something you observed in nature, then you were following the first steps of the scientific method.

FORMING A HYPOTHESIS

Scientists pose many questions and suggest possible answers. However, the scientific method demands that answers be supported by evidence.

A hypothesis is a testable answer to a question. Not all questions lead to useful hypotheses. In fact, scientists often search for just the right way to phrase a question so that they can form an hypothesis.

For example, the question "How does a caterpillar change?" is too general to lead to a hypothesis. A more specific question is "Does temperature affect how a caterpillar changes?" A hypothesis could be: Cold temperatures slow the speed that a caterpillar changes into a butterfly.

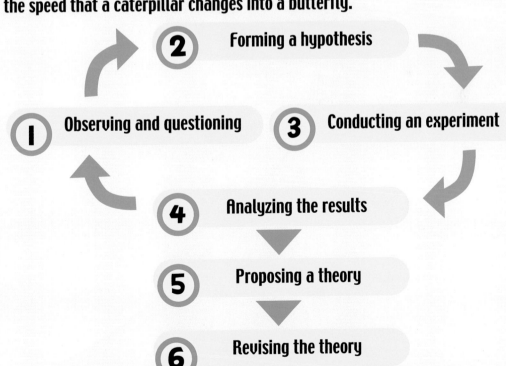

2 Forming a hypothesis

1 Observing and questioning

3 Conducting an experiment

4 Analyzing the results

5 Proposing a theory

6 Revising the theory

Conducting an experiment

To provide evidence for or against a hypothesis, scientists conduct a fair, logical test called an experiment. For example, consider the experiment illustrated in the diagram. It logically tests the hypothesis that temperature affects the speed at which caterpillars change by testing caterpillar development at different temperatures.

The experiment requires a two-part set-up, meaning two separate tests. All but one of the conditions are the same in the set-ups. Conditions kept the same are called **controls**. Here, the controls include the number of caterpillars, their food supply, and the shape and size of their containers.

Variables

In this experiment, the condition that differs is the temperature. This condition is called the **independent variable**. A useful experiment tests the effect of only one independent variable.

During the course of the experiment, the scientist observes how the caterpillars change. The scientist also keeps track of the time. Time is the **dependent variable**, which is the effect of the independent variable.

A pair of **terrariums** are needed to test the effect of temperature on caterpillars. This experiment is just an example, so do not try it yourself. It is difficult to keep caterpillars alive.

ANALYZING THE RESULTS

After 3 weeks, the caterpillars in the warm container all had become butterflies. But in the cold container, many were still in cocoons.

If you read the hypothesis again, you will see that the results provide evidence that supports it. However, the hypothesis has not been proven correct. The experiment tested only a few caterpillars under certain circumstances.

In fact, no single experiment ever completely proves a scientific idea. Results merely provide evidence for or against a hypothesis. By analyzing results, scientists often find new questions to ask and hypotheses to test.

Cold cellar 7 °C (45 °F)

start of experiment

after 3 weeks

Sunny room 24 °C (75 °F)

start of experiment

after 3 weeks

Proposing a theory

An experiment that is designed properly produces the same results every time. Scientists often repeat an experiment many times, sometimes in exactly the same way. Doing so builds up a body of evidence to support a single hypothesis or related hypotheses.

By drawing conclusions from the results of many experiments, scientists may be able to propose a theory. **A theory is a powerful explanation of events in nature, and it can be used to predict future events.** Many theories are accompanied by formulas. A **formula** is a mathematical equation. It shows a relationship or rule and relates different variables.

Many important scientific theories are hundreds of years old. In the 1600s, for example, Isaac Newton proposed theories and formulas to explain **forces**, gravity, and **motion** (the action of being moved). They remain in use to this day.

Revising theories

Scientists adopt new theories when they explain evidence better than old theories do. An example is the theory of **plate tectonics**, which reflects Alfred Wegener's ideas about moving continents. This theory replaced other theories about the way Earth changed.

In other cases, a new theory only partly replaces an older one. In 1905, for example, Albert Einstein proposed a new theory to explain time and motion. Yet it overturned Newton's theories only for special cases, when objects are moving nearly at the **speed of light** (the actual speed at which light travels). In those cases, time slows down for the object traveling at that high speed.

On the Moon, astronaut David Scott showed that a hammer and a feather fall at the same rate through empty space. He was testing an idea that was **400** years old!

TRY THIS!

FALLING FAST

In the 1600's, Galileo proposed that all objects fall at the same rate if air does not slow them down. See for yourself if this is true.

1. Drop two objects at the same time and observe which falls faster. Test a variety of objects, such as books, papers, pencils, pens, erasers, and balloons.

2. Compare your results to those of David Scott on the Moon. What variable made his test different from yours?

Answer on page 47

Sharing Ideas

Scientists are experts in many skills, including observing, asking questions, experimenting, and drawing conclusions from data. Each of these skills is a part of the scientific method.

In addition, scientists practice the skill of communicating. **By communicating ideas and findings, scientists help one another make discoveries, develop theories, and advance scientific knowledge.** Scientists communicate with one another in many ways, all of which are important to their work.

Teamwork

Scientists work in many places, including universities, museums, businesses, and government agencies. In each of these places, they work together in teams. A team may conduct experiments in a **laboratory** (a place made specially for science work), investigate animals in the wild, or design the many parts of a new airplane or other invention.

Some teams work across many locations. A trial for a new drug may take place in hospitals across the country. Predicting the weather depends on **data** from a huge number of weather stations.

Communication is the key to any successful team. By talking to one another and sharing data, team members can work together toward a common goal.

Journals and conferences

Like a magazine, a **science journal** publishes articles of interest or importance to its readers. However, the authors and readers of science journals are scientists from around the world. Scientists use journals to report on their experiments and to share new ideas. The articles are reviewed to make sure their content is accurate.

Scientists also meet in person at conferences. These meetings allow scientists to discuss ideas, ask and answer questions, and form teams for new research.

Scientists both communicate and cooperate with one another. At conferences, they meet and exchange ideas.

CONTROVERSIES IN SCIENCE

Even when new evidence has been discovered, experts continue to disagree about whether birds arose from dinosaurs.

Like people in other fields, scientists sometimes disagree with one another. Sometimes the disagreements lead to controversies. A **controversy** is a public disagreement in which neither side is convinced by the other.

In science, controversies arise when scientists analyze evidence or experiments in different ways. <u>**Controversies often continue until new evidence helps to resolve them.**</u> Some controversies have lasted for many years. Many continue to this day.

Did birds come from dinosaurs?

Paleontology is the study of ancient life. A subject of controversy in this field has been the origin of birds—where they came from and how they developed.

The controversy began in 1969, when American scientist John Ostrom revived an explanation first proposed in the 1800s. Ostrom argued that birds are the direct **descendants** (distant offspring) of dinosaurs. He cited more than 20 similarities between the two kinds of animals, including facts about their bones, teeth, and hands.

The opposing theory was that birds were close cousins of dinosaurs, but not direct descendants. Experts who backed this theory emphasized the differences between birds and dinosaurs. They also questioned how flight could have arisen from dinosaurs that lived on the ground.

Over the years, many scientists offered arguments for both sides. New fossil discoveries did little to resolve the conflict.

And the answer is...

In 2008, new technology allowed scientists to study a **protein** from a dinosaur fossil. Protein is a natural structure which is an essential part of all living things. The protein in this case proved more similar to proteins from birds than from reptiles! Yet some scientists question whether the sample was genuine. The controversy continues.

SCIENCE, TECHNOLOGY, AND SOCIETY

How does your life differ from the lives of your parents when they were your age? What was life like for your grandparents, or your great-grandparents? Developments in technology help answer these questions. Technology is the application of science skills and knowledge for a useful purpose.

Technology affects the quality of people's lives. Telephones, televisions, automobiles, and computers are examples of very popular technologies around the world. Other examples include the many tools and procedures used in medicine, architecture, engineering, and other fields.

Old and new

Some technology is very old. The ancient Chinese invented such things as the magnetic compass, fireworks, kites, paper, and the wheelbarrow. These products have changed very little, if at all, for over a thousand years.

In other cases, technology for a product develops gradually. The first automobiles, for example, were little more than open carriages with motors. Over the years, a variety of technologies improved the speed, steering, and safety of automobiles. Today, new technology is making automobiles more energy efficient, which means they will go farther on less fuel and will produce less pollution.

Benefits and drawbacks

Technology can bring many changes, and has both benefits and drawbacks. For example, few people would want to live without electricity. Yet every technology for generating electricity has drawbacks. Burning coal pollutes the air, and dams for **hydroelectric power** (power created by running water) harm the environment of a river. Nuclear power, made by splitting **radioactive** atoms, produces dangerous waste. Even an old, familiar product such as paper has drawbacks. Forests are cut down to supply people's demand for paper. Waste paper takes up space in landfills.

Advances in technology continue to change people's lives. Each brings both benefits and drawbacks.

Computers and Society

Early computers filled rooms with electric **circuitry** and glass tubes. They were large, slow, and not reliable. But in 1958, an enginneer named Jack Kirby discovered a way to build a very small electric circuit. A circuit is a closed path with electric current flowing around it. As scientists improved Kirby's invention, computers became smaller, faster, and more powerful. They also became very popular.

<u>Within the past 25 years, computers changed how people learn and communicate. They have also changed people's jobs in nearly every industry.</u> Computers are now used to track customer orders and bank accounts, design books and magazines, and build models of bridges and airplanes. People everywhere use the Internet—a huge network of computers--to communicate with text, sounds, and pictures.

Yet along with its benefits, computer technology has brought many challenges to society. Here are some of these challenges.

- ## Jobs on the move
  People can use computers and telephones to communicate all over the world. This allows employers to move many jobs to countries where wages are low. Use of computers has also eliminated many jobs.

• Privacy

Telephone numbers, street addresses, and even satellite photographs of neighborhoods are all available on the Internet to anyone in the world. Just what kinds of information should be kept private?

• Crime

Criminals are using computers, too. Some use the Internet to sell phony products or services. Others try to steal people's passwords to bank accounts or credit cards.

• Owner's rights

Writers and artists depend on the sales of books, magazines, music, and movies. But the Internet allows people to share all sorts of materials, often for no charge. How should the rights of the writer and artist be protected?

• Competition for news

The local newspaper was once the best source of news in the community. On the Internet, however, people can read the news at any time, from many sources, and free of charge. Companies are moving ads to the Internet, too.

Computers have completely changed the way we work, play, and shop. Are all of the changes for the better?

What do you think?

Computers have become key parts of everyone's daily life. Which of their benefits and drawbacks do you think are most significant?

CONFLICTS OVER TECHNOLOGY

People often disagree about the value of a new technology. **Businesses, consumers (people who buy goods), government officials, and scientists may have different interests in any new technology, as well as many opinions about it.** Sometimes those interests and opinions are in conflict.

Rows of corn will spur the growth of corn-eating beetles and other pests. Genetically-modified corn resists such pests.

Genetically-modified food

One conflict today involves new farming technology. Over the past 20 years, seed companies have been developing strains of farm crops that include genes from bacteria (single-celled microorganisms). Genes are what control inherited traits, such as having dimples. The bacterial genes help the crops fight pests. Today, much of the world's corn crop is **genetically modified**.

Seed companies insist that foods from the new crops are the same as before. However, not everyone agrees. Some people are concerned that the new foods have less nutritional value or are damaged in ways not yet understood. They argue for further study and stricter regulation (limits).

Farmers also are involved in the conflict. Many farmers do not want to raise the new crops, yet the plants can easily spread from one field to the next. Seed companies and farmers have filed lawsuits (to argue about something in court) over this issue.

Organic farming

Many farmers and consumers are choosing **alternatives** to the latest technologies. In a practice called organic farming, crops are raised without pest-killing chemicals or other special measures. Crops grow well because a variety of crops are grown side by side. This stops pests that feed on only one type of crop.

Organic farming requires more work than technology-based farming, which is why foods from organic farms can be expensive. Yet many people think that the extra cost is worthwhile.

Pests spread poorly in an organic farm, where many crops are grown together. However, organic farming involves a lot more work.

Farm debate

1. Research genetically-modified crops and people's opinions about them. Choose a specific crop, such as corn, or focus on how genetically-modified foods affect the environment. Include a variety of opinions from many sources (Internet, newspapers, TV, etc).

2. With your classmates, stage a debate on the question: Should a farmer raise genetically-modified crops? Divide into two teams, one for each side of this issue.

Making choices

Technology allows people to make choices about the way they live their lives. Because of technology, people can choose to live in suburbs and work in cities. They can buy fresh fruits and vegetables grown thousands of miles away, or buy frozen foods. They can choose from many options for their education, health care, and entertainment.

Choices and the government

Government policies often affect people's choices. Governments decide how much money to invest in highways and airports, schools and hospitals, the military, and scientific research. Policies on taxing (money given to the government by citizens) and spending can help promote new technology or help slow it down.

Policy choices often are fiercely debated. In the 2008 elections, candidates debated whether or not oil reserves in the Gulf of Mexico should be tapped. Many politicians argued that new drilling would lower the cost of gasoline. Others held that the risk of polluting the ocean was not worth the potential benefit, and that we should be reducing our dependence on oil.

People often band together to argue for or against public policies. These people are protesting against global warming. They want to see stronger reductions in air pollution.

An oil rig can tap deposits underneath the ocean floor. Many people argue that the risk of polluting ocean waters is not worth the benefit.

Your future

Scientists often voice their opinions about the choices that the public faces. Environmental scientists urge people to protect wildlife and wild places. Climate scientists argue for measures to fight global warming. They feel we must convert to clean energy. Scientists in many fields ask for public funding for their research.

You have every right to voice your opinions, too. Do you think we should drill for new oil, promote energy conservation and new technologies, or do both? What measures do you think should be taken to fight pollution? What about helping endangered species, or improving people's health and fitness?

If you are still deciding where you stand on these issues, you can learn more from science books, magazines, and Internet sites. Learning the facts about a problem is the first step in finding a solution.

Science and Ethics

Ethics are the "right and wrong" values we use to make decisions. **To achieve their goals, scientists are expected to follow high standards of ethics.** When a scientist reports on an experiment or an observation, that report is expected to be truthful and accurate. The scientist must also give appropriate credit to the work of others.

Some questions about ethics in science have clear answers. Other questions have proven more difficult and controversial.

Before a new drug is sold to the public, it must be thoroughly tested and proven to be effective.

Laws and policies

Laws and policies protect scientists and the public in their dealings with one another. Regardless of the importance of their work, scientists are expected to obey the law.

At hospitals, for example, patients have the legal right to accept or deny the treatment they receive. When patients are not physically able to agree to a treatment, their families may decide for them.

Many laws ensure that technology products are safe. New drugs and medicines must be tested and approved. Cars, bridges, buildings, and products that run on electricity must meet specific safety standards.

Laws protect the relationships among hospitals, doctors, and patients.

Stem cell research

Not everyone agrees about certain laws and the ethical values they enforce. For example, the law currently allows scientists to conduct research on human stem cells. Stem cells are cells in the very early stages of development. Cells are the smallest units of life. The law does not allow scientists to harvest (gather) new strains, or varieties, of stem cells.

Scientists and the public continue to debate the ethics of stem cell research. Critics argue that stem cells should never be harvested, as they are a form of human life. Others dispute this claim. They also emphasize that stem cell research could lead to cures for many diseases.

The rights of animals

Scientists often study animals and conduct experiments on them. Medicines, foods, and health care products are tested on animals before they are given to humans. Surgeons may practice on animals or run experiments on them. **Psychologists** study animal behavior as a way to learn about human behavior.

Many animals do not survive their experience in science research. Yet the research can help people all over the world.

Laws protect animals from being treated cruelly. Yet is it ethical to conduct research on animals? Before you answer, consider the many sides of this question. Humans have befriended some animals, such as dogs and cats. Should scientists treat these animals differently from ones that are considered pests, such as rats, mice, and some insects? Do humanitarian (for the good of human kind) goals make animal research ethical? Or is any research acceptable as long as it causes no pain to the animals? Is it possible to cause no pain to the animals?

Scientists, lawmakers, and public-interest groups often discuss questions such as these. **Many questions of ethics are quite complex and difficult to answer.** Often, no answer is completely right or wrong. Sometimes an answer only raises further questions.

Ethical questions

Consider these topics and questions. None have simple answers that everyone agrees upon.

- **Death and dying:** Sometimes doctors can prolong the life of a dying patient. When should a patient no longer be treated and be allowed to die?

- **Public health: Vaccines** help prevent disease, but they also carry certain risks. Should parents be required to have their children vaccinated? Or is it a personal choice?

- **Dangerous knowledge:** During World War II, scientists working for the United States developed the **atomic bomb.** Such bombs were—and remain—extremely powerful weapons. Should new scientific knowledge always be pursued?

SCIENCE, CULTURE, AND VALUES

Nature has always affected people's lives. People depend on plants and animals for food. Weather and climate affect crops and livestock. Storms, diseases, and pests have caused trouble throughout history, just as they do today.

Stonehenge may have served ancient people as an **observatory**. People have been striving to understand nature for thousands of years.

Many faiths and **cultural traditions** provide explanations of nature, often in the form of stories or histories. <u>Sometimes, explanations from faith and culture conflict with those from science.</u> Many conflicts arose and were settled in the past. Others remain active today.

Galileo and the moving Earth

The work of Galileo is one example of a conflict between faith and science. Galileo was an Italian scientist of the early 1600s, when the Pope and the Catholic church held much power.

Galileo built new kinds of telescopes for studying the night sky. He made many discoveries with his telescopes, among them that Venus has phases much like Moon phases. He applied these discoveries to argue a new idea: that the Earth and other planets moved in space around the Sun.

Unfortunately for Galileo, the Pope of this time deemed a Sun-centered system to be completely against the church's teachings. Galileo was arrested and forced to deny his work. His books were banned, which meant anyone reading them could be punished.

Over time, however, evidence mounted in support of Galileo's ideas. Eventually, people everywhere accepted that the Sun, not the Earth, was the center of a system in space. In 1992, Pope John Paul II officially acknowledged that Galileo had been correct.

Galileo concluded that Earth moved through space around the Sun. The idea was heresy at first, then gradually accepted.

Contributions from science

In 1900, an average citizen of the United States lived to about age 47. A journey across the country took several days by train, while simple messages could be sent quickly over telegraph wires. Wood-burning stoves provided heat in winter, while waving a paper fan was a simple way to stay cool in summer.

Since then, advancements in science have changed people's lives dramatically. **Scientists have made huge contributions to people's culture and quality of life.** The contributions listed below are only three examples.

Electricity

Light bulbs, air conditioners, and computers are only a few of the inventions that depend on electricity. They allow people to gather together at night, to communicate around the world, and to live comfortably even in the hottest climates.

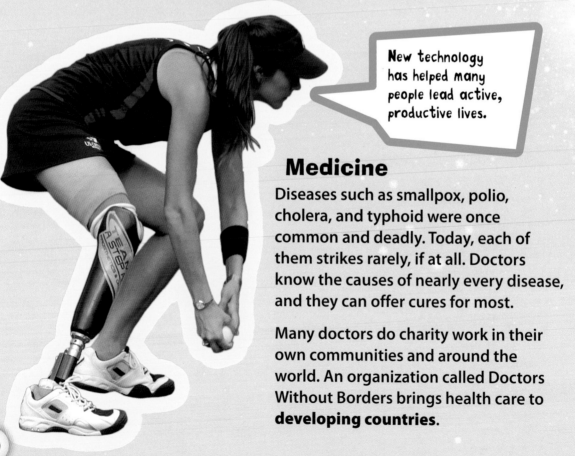

New technology has helped many people lead active, productive lives.

Medicine

Diseases such as smallpox, polio, cholera, and typhoid were once common and deadly. Today, each of them strikes rarely, if at all. Doctors know the causes of nearly every disease, and they can offer cures for most.

Many doctors do charity work in their own communities and around the world. An organization called Doctors Without Borders brings health care to **developing countries**.

EXPLORING SPACE

In the 1950s and 1960s, the United States and the Soviet Union competed fiercely to send astronauts into space. Today, the United States, Russia, and other countries are cooperating in space exploration.

Space missions show what humans are capable of accomplishing. They also inspire people to think about global issues, such as the importance of keeping Earth a healthy home for humankind.

Greg Chamitoff, USA

Oleg Kononenko, Russia

Servei Volkov, Russia

Astronauts from many countries are working to complete the International Space Station. People around the world take pride in their accomplishments.

The Conflict Over EVOLUTION

How did life on Earth begin? How did plants, animals, and other living things come to be? People have long wondered about questions like these. Sometimes they look to their faith and religious traditions for answers.

Scientists also wonder about the origin of life. <u>A scientific theory, however, must be based on evidence from nature, not stories or books.</u>

Charles Darwin

In the 1800s, English scientist Charles Darwin proposed the theory of evolution. The theory is that new species (types) arose gradually, or evolved, from earlier species. Darwin's evidence included observations of fossils and living animals.

Since Darwin's time, scientists have discovered a lot of evidence in support of evolution. Many predictions based on the theory have proven correct. Yet the theory continues to spark public debate, just as it did in Darwin's time.

Today, opponents of evolution argue that life is too complex to have evolved. They believe that each species, or kind of living thing, must have been created or designed. They also claim their ideas should be accepted as a scientific theory called intelligent design. In response, many scientists dismiss these claims as lacking any scientific basis (evidence).

According to the theory of evolution, fossils are evidence that species changed over time. Opponents of evolution argue that such changes are not possible.

LAWS, SCHOOLS, AND COURTS

People have debated evolution before legislators, school boards, and judges. States present evolution in a variety of ways in their education standards. Evolution is taught extensively in some public schools, and not at all in others.

In 2005, a judge in Pennsylvania ruled that intelligent design was a religious idea, not a scientific theory. He barred its teaching in local schools. Although the case was not appealed (brought back to court), the issue likely will arise in U.S. courts again.

How should you spend the money you have? How can you earn more money? Everyone faces these questions. So do universities, businesses, and governments. All three employ scientists or sponsor the work of scientists.

<u>Like everyone else, scientists are expected to produce work that justifies its cost.</u> Economics affect the type of work that scientists do, as well as the quality of that work. Below are some examples.

Economics at the hospital

Doctors work hard to provide the best health care for their patients. Yet this often means taking economic factors into account. An expensive drug may not be the best choice for a patient who cannot afford it. An extra day in the hospital might improve a patient's health, but the cost may not be worth the benefit.

Today, most Americans have insurance that pays for some of their medical expenses, but not all of them. Insurance companies follow strict rules for what they will and will not pay for.

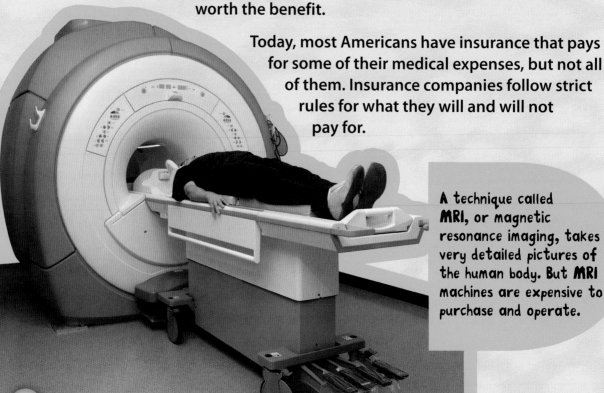

A technique called **MRI**, or magnetic resonance imaging, takes very detailed pictures of the human body. But **MRI** machines are expensive to purchase and operate.

Economics of scientific research

Scientific research can be expensive. Salaries, travel, and laboratory equipment must all be paid for. Some projects take years to complete.

Fortunately, many institutions are interested in funding research projects. Drug companies, airplane manufacturers, and agricultural businesses hire research scientists to develop new products. The U.S. government grants money for research in many fields.

Typically, organizations that fund scientific research expect a return on their investment. Scientists whose research is profitable (makes money) usually find funding easy to secure.

Scientific research is often expensive. If the research is not going to develop something that will make money, it might not be funded.

Large Collider, Huge Cost

In 2008, CERN (the European Organization for Nuclear Research) finished building the Large Hadron Collider (LHC) the world's largest particle accelerator. The LHC will use high speeds to smash particles together, and this will provide information for physics research. It is hoped that the 27 kilometer (17 mile) long, underground facility will help physicists make many new discoveries about our world and even the universe. Especially since it cost $8 billion, $531 million of which was contributed by the United States!

Economics and energy

In the early 1970s, a gallon of gasoline cost drivers around 30 or 40 cents. By 2008, that cost had increased ten times over. Economists explain this increase in terms of supply and demand. Because the world's supply of gasoline decreased while demand for it rose, the price rose as well.

Gasoline is made from petroleum, which is a type of **fossil fuel** (a natural fuel formed from the remains of living things over very long periods of time). Today, much scientific research is focused on developing alternatives to fossil fuels. One alternative is ethanol, a fuel made from plants. Another is the **hydrogen fuel cell**, which combines hydrogen and oxygen for fuel. There are also power plants driven by energy from the Sun, wind, and tides.

Scientists have proposed many ideas for developing alternative energy sources. The ideas include building wind farms in the ocean and installing solar panels in deserts (to take advantage of the intense sunlight). Whether or not such proposals are acted upon are decisions for businesses, the government, and the general public.

As fossil fuels become more expensive, investors become more interested in developing alternative energy sources. These sources include wind, solar, and geothermal (heat from the earth) power.

Hidden costs

As scientists have concluded, many products have hidden costs that are not reflected in their price. This is especially true for fuels and electricity.

Burning gasoline pollutes the air and can cause **acid rain**. Acid rain can damage wildlife, as well as human-made structures. Hydroelectric dams (dams that make electricity from flowing water) harm river animals and affect life downstream. **Nuclear power plants** produce radioactive waste that is dangerous and needs to be carefully stored for many years. Few people include such costs when they evaluate these sources of energy.

This car does not run on gasoline. It uses batteries that generate electricity! Such cars may soon become more economical and popular.

Energy table

1. Imagine that a power company wants to build a new plant to serve your community. Research an energy source for this plant, such as nuclear, hydroelectric, wind, solar, geothermal, or coal.

2. Create a table showing the advantages and disadvantages of each source. Then stage a debate with classmates about which energy source would work best. Support your position with the table, and other facts and evidence.

GLOBAL CLIMATE CHANGE

Global climate change may be the most important issue that society has ever faced. The issue is also quite complex. It combines matters of science, technology, politics (the actions and people in governments), and economics.

Many scientists raised the possibility of climate change in the 1980s, and some raised it even earlier. Although experts debated at first, they now agree almost completely. **By burning fossil fuels and cutting down forests, humans are raising the levels of carbon dioxide gas in Earth's atmosphere. This is causing a global rise in temperature.**

In 2007, an international team of climate scientists predicted that global temperatures could rise over 6° C by the end of the century. This rise would be enough to melt polar ice, raise ocean levels, and change weather patterns across the planet. These events have already begun to happen.

Climate change might even increase the strength of hurricanes. This image shows Hurricane Ike hitting Galveston, Texas in September of **2008**.

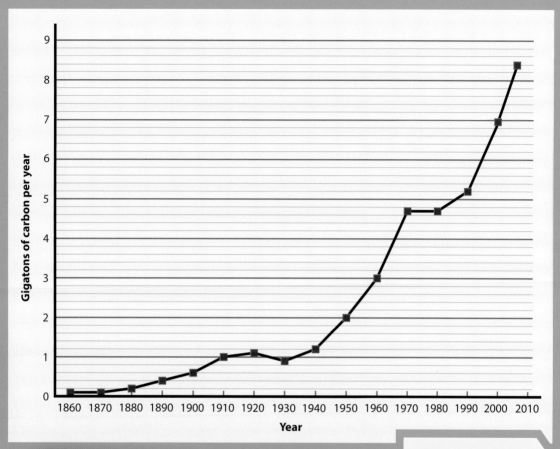

Take a look at this graph. People have been using more carbon every year. People everywhere will need to take action for this trend to change.

Solving the problem

Scientists argue that climate change might not be stoppable, but it can be slowed down. The key is to lower the levels of carbon dioxide.

How can this be done? Scientists, environmental groups, and some government leaders have been urging people to take several steps.

- **Invest in new technology** The use of most alternative sources of energy does not produce carbon dioxide.
- **Conserve energy** If people use less electricity or other energy products, fewer fossil fuels are needed.
- **Pass new laws** Limits should be placed on the volume of carbon dioxide that enters the atmosphere.
- **Protect forests and plant trees** In one year, a mature tree could take in 48 pounds of carbon dioxide from the air.
- **Work together** Climate change affects people in every country. Everyone must be part of the solution.

A reluctance to act

Climate scientists have amassed huge volumes of **data**, and their explanations of climate and weather patterns are widely accepted. People can also observe the effects of climate change with their own eyes. These effects include glaciers melting, ice caps breaking apart, and shorter spans of winter weather.

So why are many people reluctant to take action against climate change? Some deny that human actions are causing climate change, or even that climate change is possible. Others cite the expense of switching away from fossil fuels. People also value their freedom and independence, and don't like others deciding what is best for them.

Unfortunately, the longer people delay the fight against climate change, the worse its effects will be. Decisions made today will affect the world for years to come.

Evidence for global climate change comes from many sources, including the layers of ice in polar ice caps.

You can help!

You can help solve any problem—including climate change—by learning as much as you can about it. Then you can share your knowledge and opinions with friends, family, and the community.

You also can take actions that make a difference. Walk, bike, or take public transportation when possible. Turn off electrical appliances when they are not in use. Plant trees, especially when old trees fall down. These steps may be small, but they are part of the solution to a very big problem.

Switching to alternative energy sources, such as energy from the Sun, is an important step in slowing global climate change.

Summary

Science issues and controversies arise because the work of scientists affects the way people live and how they think about the world.

- Science relies on the scientific method, an organized process that involves the skills of observing, questioning, experimenting, and analyzing data.

- A theory is a powerful explanation of events in nature, and it can be used to predict future events.

- Controversies arise among scientists as they do within other disciplines. Different scientists may interpret evidence or analyze data in different ways.

- Technology is the application of science to a practical use. Computers and other new technology bring both benefits and drawbacks to people's lives.

- Genetically-modified food, such as frost-resistant strawberries, is an example of a controversial technology. People have different opinions about its value.

- Scientists are expected to follow high standards of ethics and to obey the law. Scientists and the public often debate ethical issues, such as stem cell research and the rights of animals.

- As with Darwin's theory of evolution, scientific theories sometimes conflict with other ideas about nature.

- Economic factors affect much of the work that scientists do. As the cost of fossil fuels rises, for example, more money is invested in developing alternative energy sources.

- Solving the problem of global climate change involves science, technology, politics, and economics. It may be the most important issue that society has ever faced.

What did you learn?

1 **Which step comes first in the scientific method?**
a. forming an hypothesis
b. analyzing data
c. observing and asking questions
d. developing a theory

2 **Which is most likely to resolve a disagreement or controversy among scientists?**
a. new evidence that supports one side
b. new government laws or policies
c. public opinion
d. a vote among scientists

3 **Paper, automobiles, computers, and electrical power plants are each examples of technology that __ .**
a. brings benefits only
b. brings benefits and drawbacks
c. has changed very little over time
d. has changed greatly over time

4 **Today, the public continues to debate the ethics of __ .**
a. the scientific method
b. a Sun-centered solar system
c. organic farming
d. stem cell research

5 **What did Galileo's model of the solar system have in common with Darwin's theory of evolution?**
a. both were quickly and widely accepted
b. both were proven false
c. both raised conflicts with people's faiths
d. both were proposed during the same year

6 **Climate change is a problem that is facing __ .**
a. scientists only
b. Americans and Europeans only
c. politicians only
d. everyone all over the world

Check your answers on page 47!

Glossary

acid rain rainfall that is acidic enough to damage the environment

alternative option apart from normal or popular choices

atomic bomb powerful weapon that harnesses the energy of atomic nuclei, or the inner cores of atoms

circuitry set of wires used to carry electricity

control condition kept the same among the tested groups of an experiment

controversy public disagreement in which neither side is convinced by the other

cultural traditions customs, practices, or beliefs within a culture, or social group

data set of factual observations or measurements

dependent variable effect of the independent variable

descendant offspring of any degree of remoteness, such as a child, or grandchild, great-grandchild

developing country relatively poor country that is becoming more prosperous

ethics difference between right and wrong

evidence observable fact or set of facts from nature

evolution idea that species arise from earlier species

experiment fair, logical test of an hypothesis

force push or a pull

formula mathematical equation that relates different variables in nature

fossil fuel high-energy substance, such as coal or oil, that formed from the remains of ancient life

genetically modified carrying genes that scientists directly altered

hydroelectric power electricity produced by water running over a dam

hydrogen fuel cell battery-like device that runs on hydrogen

hypothesis testable answer to a question

independent variable variable that the experiment alters among the test groups

intelligent design the claim that species must have been individually created, or designed

laboratory room or other environment for conducting scientific experiments or research

meteorologist scientist who studies the weather

motion movement

nuclear power plant facility where electricity is produced from the energy of atoms' nuclei, or inner cores

observatory station or building designed for observing stars, planets, and other objects in space

plate tectonics theory that Earth's outer surface is divided into large, slow-moving sections, or plates

protein class of compounds used by all living things

psychologist scientist or doctor who studies how people think and behave

radioactive releasing energy due to changes in atomic nuclei, the inner cores of atoms

science inquiry *see scientific method*

science journal publication that allows scientists to share and evaluate ideas and discoveries

scientific method system of observation, experimentation, and analysis that leads to a logical conclusion. Also called science inquiry.

speed of light extremely fast speed that a light ray travels at

technology application of science skills and knowledge for a useful purpose

terrarium container that holds soil and a variety of plants, and may act as a model of Earth

theory powerful explanation of events in nature, which can be used to predict future events

vaccine treatment that prepares the body for fighting a specific disease

variable condition that differs among the tested groups of an experiment

Find Out More

Books

Christianson, Gale E. ***Isaac Newton and the Scientific Revolution***. New York: Oxford University Press, 1996.

Coad, John. ***Reducing Pollution***. Chicago: Heinmann Library, 2009.

Flowers, Sarah. ***Space Exploration: A Pro/Con Issue***. Berkely Heights, NJ: Enslow Publishers, 2000.

Judson, Karen. ***Medical Ethics: Life and Death Issues***. Berkely Heights, NJ: Enslow Publishers, 2001.

Morgan, Sally. ***Alternative Energy Sources***. Chicago: Heinemann Library, 2009.

Nye, Bill. ***Bill Nye the Science Guy's Big Blast of Science***. New York: Harper Collins, 2006.

Torr, James D. ***Current Controversies: The Information Age***. Farmington Hills, MI: Greenhaven Press, 2002.

Websites

Newton's Apple
http://www.newtonsapple.tv/
This website is devoted to science knowledge and exploration.

Try Science.org
http://www.tryscience.org/home.html
Try Science is your gateway to exploring science and technology.

EERE Kids: About Renewable Energy
http://www.eere.energy.gov/kids/renergy.html
Discover the advantages and disadvantages of renewable energy resources.

Places to visit

A day at the science museum is fun and educational. Visit the science museum in your community, or try these museums online.

Boston Museum of Science
1 Science Park
Boston, MA 02114
http://www.mos.org

Exploratorium: the Museum of Science, Art, and Human Preception
3601 Lyon Street
San Francisco, CA 94123
http://www.exploratorium.edu/

Museum of Science and Industry
57th and Lake Shore Drive
Chicago, IL 60637
http://www.msichicago.org

National Museum of Natural History
10th Street & Constitution Avenue NW
Washington, D.C. 20560
http://www.mnh.si.edu

Answer to question on page 11

The variable is air, as there is no air on the Moon.

Answers to quiz on page 43

1. c, 2. a, 3. b, 4. d, 5. c, 6. d.

Index